INVESTIGATE! HIGH GEAR

# MUSTANGS

Enslow PUBLISHING

THERESA EMMINIZER

**Please visit our website, www.enslow.com.**
**For a free color catalog of all our high-quality books, call toll free 1-800-398-2504 or fax 1-877-980-4454.**

**Library of Congress Cataloging-in-Publication Data**
Names: Emminizer, Theresa.
Title: Mustangs / Theresa Emminizer.
Description: New York : Enslow Publishing, 2023. | Series: High Gear | Includes glossary and index.
Identifiers: ISBN 9781978528666 (pbk.) | ISBN 9781978528680 (library bound) | ISBN 9781978528697 (ebook)
Subjects: LCSH: Mustang automobile–Juvenile literature.
Classification: LCC TL215.M8 E46 2023 | DDC 629.222–dc23

Published in 2023 by
**Enslow Publishing**
2544 Clinton Street
Buffalo, NY 14224



Portions of this work were originally authored by Seth Kingston and published as *The History of Mustangs*. All new material in this edition is authored by Theresa Emminizer.

Designer: Leslie Taylor
Editor: Theresa Emminizer

Photo credits: Cover (car) Darren Brode/Shutterstock.com; Series Art (background swooshes) NAAN/Shutterstock.com; Series Art (sport alphabet) geen graphy/Shutterstock.com; Series Art (banner) Natykach Nataliia/Shutterstock.com; p. 5 Nor Gal/Shuttertstock.com; p. 7 Roman Belogorodov/Shutterstock.com; p. 9 Rob Wilson/Shutterstock.com; p. 11 Bruce Alan Bennett/Shutterstock.com; p. 13 Steve Lagreca/Shutterstock.com; p.15 Jeff Bukowski/Shutterstock.com; p.17 Grzegorz Czapski/Shutterstock.com; p.19 Grzegorz Czapski/Shutterstock.com; p.21 Roman Belogorodov/Shutterstock.com; p.23 Clari Massimiliano/Shutterstock.com; p.25 GEORGE STAMATIS/Shutterstock.com; p.27 (Shelby) Sicnag, https://commons.wikimedia.org/wiki/File:1965_Shelby_Mustang_GT350_(20984175008).jpg, (SVO) Jimnva, https://commons.wikimedia.org/wiki/File:86_SVO.jpg; p.29 https://commons.wikimedia.org/wiki/File:2021_Ford_Mustang_Fastback_2.3L_%2851767449779%29.jpg.



Printed in the United States of America

CPSIA compliance information: Batch #CWENS23: For further information contact Enslow Publishing at 1-800-398-2504.

# CONTENTS



Words in the glossary appear in **bold** type the first time they are used in the text.

# Mustangs On Top

Mustangs are American classics. Made by Ford, a company that's known for its many **innovations** and for shaping American history, this car has been popular since it first came out in 1964. In 1965, a white **convertible** Mustang was even placed on the observation deck of the Empire State Building! It stayed there for five months until it was taken down on March 16, 1966.

From the 1960s to present day, Mustangs have captured the hearts and imaginations of American car lovers. Their one-of-a-kind style and power sets them apart.

The Mustang logo, or identifying image, pictures a running horse.

## Explore More!

The Ford Motor Company was founded in 1903 by Henry Ford. In 1913, Ford introduced the **assembly line** to auto production, making car manufacturing faster and easier. It was the first company to do so. Today, almost all cars are made on assembly lines.

# The First Pony Car

Historically, European car manufacturers such as Alfa Romeo, Ferrari, and Lamborghini led sports car production. But that changed when two Ford employees, Lee Iacocca and Donald Frey, came up with the idea of a pony car!

A pony car is a smaller two-door car with sporty styling and high performance, or operation. Unlike other sports cars, it had a back seat. The Mustang's back seat and large trunk made it much more practical, or useful, than European sports cars. It had enough space for a small family and their bags and gear.

## Explore More!

The Ford Mustang was one of the first pony cars. By 1969, many other American car manufacturers had their own versions, or kinds, of a pony car. Other pony cars include the Pontiac Firebird, the Chevrolet Camaro, the Plymouth Barracuda, and the Dodge Challenger.

Pony cars usually cost less than many European sports cars.

# Selling Fast!

The Mustang was named after the P-51 Mustang fighter plane from World War II. Ford introduced the Mustang at the New York World's Fair on April 17, 1964. It was **designed** to be an affordable, **customizable** sports car for the average American car lover. When the Mustang made its debut, or first appearance, it cost just $2,368.

Ford hoped to sell 100,000 Mustangs in the first year. The company sold 22,000 Mustangs on the first day! In the car's first 18 months, Ford sold about 500,000 Mustangs.

The Mustang is one of the fastest-selling cars in history.

## Explore More!

Part of what makes Mustangs so popular is that they've been featured in many movies and on TV. The Mustang has appeared in the movies ***Ford vs. Ferrari***, ***I Am Legend***, and many others.

# Mustangs in Motorsport

Very shortly after its debut at the World's Fair, a Mustang served as the **pace car** for the 1964 Indianapolis 500. Mustangs then took first and second place in their class in the international 1964 Tour de France rally.

In American racing, the Mustang made its debut in drag racing. In drag racing, cars race next to each other in a straight line. Some National Hot Rod Association (NHRA) teams race Mustangs. Hot rods are cars that are rebuilt or changed to be faster. The NHRA is a drag-racing organization.

A Mustang pulls a wheelie while leaving the start line during a **vintage** drag racing event.

## Explore More!

Mustangs have also raced in National Association for Stock Car Auto Racing (NASCAR) races. A stock car is a race car that's based on an existing production car. NASCAR is the most popular racing series in the United States.

# The 1964½ Mustang

A generation is the life cycle of a certain make and model of a car. The first generation of Mustangs debuted in 1964, but these cars were sold as 1965 models. The cars built between April and August 1964 are often called 1964½ Mustangs, but they belong to the 1965 model year.

1964½ Mustangs had a different electrical system and a smaller V-8 engine then 1965 models. The 1964½ came as a convertible or a **coupe**. Other options included a six-**cylinder** (V-6) engine with 101 **horsepower** (hp) or a V-8 engine with 210 hp.

Only 121,538 of the 1964½ models were produced.

## Explore More!

Mustangs were sold as "the car to be designed by you." They could be as plain or as fancy as a buyer wished. Buyers could choose between different colors, interiors (inner parts), exteriors (outer parts), and transmissions, which transfer power from a car's engine to its wheels.

# The Bullitt

The 1968 GT 390 Fastback is possibly the most famous Mustang of all time. That's partly because it was featured in the movie *Bullitt*, which came out that year. Two Mustang GT 390 Fastbacks were modified, or changed, to make the movie car. Only one is still around today.

*Bullitt* showed a 9-minute and 42-second car chase. The scene was filmed as though watchers were inside the Mustang, driving down real roads in San Francisco, California. There was no dialogue, or talking, in this famous part of the movie.

The movie Bullitt car is the dark highland green color. Later, when special-edition Bullitts were made, that would still be the most popular color choice.

## Explore More!

GT stands for grand touring, which is a sporty car made for long trips.

# Ford Mustang II

The second generation of Mustangs were made from 1974 until 1978. These were called the Ford Mustang II. They only came as a hatchback or coupe.

In the first year, the Mustang II had the option of a four-cylinder, 92-horsepower engine or a V-6, 105-horsepower engine. In 1975, Ford reintroduced the option of a V-8 engine. The engine also came in two sizes, 2.3 liters or 2.8 liters. However, this Mustang still wasn't as powerful as other sports cars at the time and had a top speed of only around 99 miles (159 km) per hour.

A hatchback is a car with a back door that opens upward.

## Explore More!

The Mustang II was introduced at a turning point in the car manufacturing industry. In response to the changing times, Ford redesigned the Mustang. The Mustang II's design is based on the design of the Ford Pinto.

# The Fox Body Mustang

The third generation Mustang is called the Fox or Fox Body Mustang. It was larger and lighter than the Mustang II and looked more like European sports cars.

The Fox Body Mustang had a new running horse logo and four headlights. The 1979 model was available with a 2.3-liter four-cylinder engine, a 2.8-liter V-6, a 3.3-liter six-cylinder, or a 5.0-liter V-8 engine. In 1987, the Fox Body was redesigned to have more **aerodynamic** headlights, a smoother nose, and black exterior parts. It was also available with a 2.3-liter four-cylinder or 5.0-liter V-8 engine.

The Fox Body was available as a coupe or a hatchback.

## Explore More!

The 1979 Mustang was chosen as the pace car for that year's Indianapolis 500. To celebrate, or honor, this car, Ford produced 11,000 "Official Pace Car" hatchbacks.

# The Anniversary Editions

The fourth generation of Mustangs were introduced in 1994, the year Ford celebrated 30 years of making Mustangs. The 1994 Mustang had a 3.8-liter V-6 engine that produced 145 horsepower.

Ford redesigned the Mustang again for its 35th **anniversary** in 1999. In 2003, Ford produced its 300 millionth car, a red 2004 Mustang GT convertible.

In 2004, Ford produced a 40th anniversary edition. It was available as a coupe or convertible version of the standard and GT models. The package included special exterior and interior changes.

In 1994 Ford stopped making the Fox Body and came up with a new design for the fourth generation, shown above.

## Explore More!

**Ford produced 4,628 limited-edition Mustang GTs to celebrate its 35th anniversary in 1999. The new Mustang had sharper lines, larger wheel arches, and a more powerful engine with 190 horsepower. It came in red, black, silver, or white.**

# Faster and More Powerful

Mustang's fifth generation cars were made from 2005 until 2014. These Mustangs got a new 4.0-liter V-6 engine that produced 210 horsepower.

In 2011, Ford reintroduced the Mustang Boss 302. The original Mustang Boss was made in 1979 and 1980. The 2012 Boss 302 was low to the ground and very aerodynamic. It had a V-8 engine that produced 444 horsepower. The Boss could go from 0 to 60 miles (0 to 96.6 km) per hour in about 4 seconds and had a top speed of 155 miles (249.5 km) per hour.

The fifth generation's style looked more like older generation Mustangs.

## Explore More!

In 2006, Ford introduced the Mustang GT/CS, which stands for California Special. The original California Special Mustang was made in 1968. The Mustang GT/CS had a design that looked somewhat like the 2007-2008 Shelby GT.

# 50 Years of Mustangs

In 2015, Mustang marked 50 years in production. To celebrate, Ford made a special edition of the 2015 Mustang. There were only 1,964 Mustang 50-Year Limited Edition Fastbacks produced.

To keep the sixth generation stylish, Ford used design ideas from early Mustangs in a modern way. Sixth-generation Mustangs are longer, lower, and wider than fifth-generation Mustangs. Like other generations before it, the sixth-generation Mustang is highly customizable. According to Ford, one of its goals is to allow the customer to keep their Mustang more affordable or make it as flashy as they would like.

Mustang buyers are offered many options to choose from with the sixth generation.

## Explore More!

There are three engine options for the sixth-generation Mustangs: a 2.3-liter four-cylinder, a 3.7-liter V-6, and a 5.0-liter V-8. There are also different interior options, wheel combinations, performance features, and sound system options.

# Special Editions

Throughout the years, Ford has made many special-edition Mustangs. Two that stand out are the Shelby and the SVO. The Shelby was named for its creator, Carroll Shelby. It was released in 1965 and produced until 1970. The Shelby GT350 helped make a name for Mustang by being a leading car in many road races. The GT350s made in 1965 and 1966 were the lightest models and are sometimes called Cobras.

The Mustang SVO was introduced in 1984. Only 4,508 SVOs were made. At the time, it was the fastest Mustang available.

# Stand-Out Specials

### Car: 1965 Shelby Mustang GT350

Engine: V-8
Horsepower: 306 hp
Top Speed: 138 miles (222 km) per hour

(1986 model)

### Car: 1984 SVO

Engine: Turbo 4-cylinder
Horsepower: 175 hp
Top Speed: About 134 miles (215.7 km) per hour

Today, the most expensive Mustangs are often Shelby GTs.

## Explore More!

The King Cobra Mustang is another stand-out special edition Mustang. It was released in 1978 and only 4,313 cars were produced. The 1978 King Cobra featured a V-8 engine. It also had a picture of a cobra snake on the hood!

# Mustangs Today

If you check out Mustang's latest lineup, you'll see the word "EcoBoost" pop up many times. Ford pioneered, or was the first to make and use, EcoBoost engines. EcoBoost engines are small and fuel-efficient, meaning they use less gas but are still powerful. EcoBoost engines were first released in 2010 models.

What's in store for the seventh generation of Mustangs? There's no release date as of mid-2022, so they may not roll out until the 2024 model year. What we know now is only that the newest Mustangs promise to offer fuel-efficient power and updated designs.

## Explore More!

Torque is the measure of the force that causes an object to rotate, or spin. In the United States, torque is usually talked about in pounds per feet. More torque means a car can accelerate, or speed up, faster.

2021 Mustang EcoBoost Fastback

# 2022 Models

**Car: Mustang EcoBoost Fastback**
Engine: 2.3 L EcoBoost
Horsepower: 310 hp
Torque: 350 lb/ft (474 Newton/meter [Nm])

**Car: Mustang EcoBoost Convertible**
Engine: 2.3 L EcoBoost
Horsepower: 310 hp
Torque: 350 lb/ft (474 Nm)

**Car: Mustang GT Fastback**
Engine: 5.0 L EcoBoost
Horsepower: 450 hp
Torque: 420 lb/ft (569 Nm)

These are just a few of the many options currently available to Mustang buyers, as of 2022.

# GLOSSARY

**aerodynamic:** Able to move through the air easily.

**anniversary:** The date on which an event took place in a previous year.

**assembly line:** A system of machines and workers in which work passes down the line step by step until the product is completed.

**convertible:** A type of car with a removable roof.

**coupe:** A type of passenger car that usually only has two doors.

**customizable:** Able to be changed to suit someone's preferences.

**cylinder:** A car part that runs the car's engine. The more cylinders a car has, the more powerful it is.

**design:** The pattern or shape of something. Also, to create the pattern or shape of something.

**horsepower:** The measure of a car's engine power.

**innovation:** A new idea.

**pace car:** In a race, the car that leads all the race cars around the track for a warm-up lap and pulls off before the race starts.

**vintage**: Something from the past, especially something that is still considered valuable.

# FOR MORE INFORMATION

## BOOKS

Mason, Paul. *Dodge, Chevrolet, Ford.* New York, NY: PowerKids Press, 2019.

Rendle, Steve. *Race Cars.* New York, NY: PowerKids Press, 2022.

Rendle, Steve. *Sports Cars.* New York, NY: PowerKids Press, 2022.

## WEBSITES

**Ford**
*corporate.ford.com/about/history.html*
Learn more about the history of the Ford Motor Company.

**Ford Mustang**
*www.ford.com/mustang/*
Check out today's Mustangs.

**Kiddle**
*kids.kiddle.co/Ford_Mustang*
Read more about the history of the Mustang.

# INDEX